P9-AQO-190

DATE DUE AUG 1 7 2004

SEP 0 2 2004			
SEP 1 4 2004			

MARTIN COUNTY LIBRARY, FL

DEMCO 38-296

FLASHY fantastic RAIN FOREST FROGS

Dorothy Hinshaw Patent

Illustrations by Kendahl Jan Jubb

Walker and Company
New York

To the memory of my brother, Bill, and sister, Barbara, who both believed in transformation of the spirit. —D. H. P.

To my parents, Myra and Jim, with fond affection.—K. J. J.

The author and artist wish to thank Jack Kover and Jeff Hall of the National Aquarium in Baltimore, Maryland, and Sam Manno for their help with this project.

Text copyright © 1997 by Dorothy Hinshaw Patent
Illustrations copyright © 1997 by Kendahl Jan Jubb

All rights reserved. No part of this book may be reproduced or transmitted in any form or by any means, electronic or mechanical, including photocopying, recording, or by any information storage and retrieval system, without permission in writing from the Publisher.

First published in the United States of America in 1997 by Walker Publishing Company, Inc.; first paperback edition published in 1999

Published simultaneously in Canada by Thomas Allen & Son Canada, Limited, Markham, Ontario

Library of Congress Cataloging-in-Publication Data
Patent, Dorothy Hinshaw.
  Flashy fantastic rain forest frogs/Dorothy Hinshaw Patent;
illustrations by Kendahl Jan Jubb.
  p. cm.
  Includes index.
  Summary: Describes the physical characteristics, behavior, reproduction, and habitat of frogs that live in the rain forest.
    ISBN 0—8027—8615—4 (hardcover).
  —ISBN 0—8027—8616—2 (reinforced)
  1. Frogs—Tropics—Juvenile literature. 2. Rain forest animals—Juvenile literature
. [1. Frogs. 2. Rain forest animals.]
I. Jubb, Kendahl Jan, ill. II. Title.
QL668.E2P36 1997
597.8—dc20
ISBN 0-8027-7536-5 (paperback)
                                                    96-29060
                                                        CIP
                                                         AC

The illustrations in this book were painted with Windsor & Newton Watercolour on Arches Watercolour Block. The text type was set in Adriatic with display type in Zinjaro by Mspace. Designed by Maura Fadden Rosenthal. Printed and bound by Colorprint Offset, Hong Kong, on 140 GSM coated offset paper.

Printed in Hong Kong
10 9 8 7 6 5 4

Flashy and fantastic—that's what rain forest frogs are. They aren't just green or brown like ordinary frogs. They can be blue or orange. They may have red stripes or bright pink bellies. Some are smaller than your thumb, and others are as big as kittens. They look different from frogs near your home. But in important ways, they are the same. Like all frogs, they have moist skin, big eyes, and long hind legs. The males croak to attract females, which then lay eggs without shells.

3

The tropical rain forest is a very special place. It never freezes. Instead of summer and winter, the rain forest has a wet and a dry season. Even during the dry season, it often rains.

The rain forest looks like a tropical garden. Plants grow everywhere, even on other plants. At the top of the rain forest is the canopy, where trees spread their leaves to gather sunlight. Below the canopy is the understory. The understory is made up of tree trunks, vines, and bushes. The forest floor is shaded by the plants above, so, often, little grows there.

5

Many frogs live in the canopy and the understory. They may never come down to the ground. Their legs are long and thin for climbing from branch to branch. Their toes have wide sticky tips that help them cling to the branches and leaves. Other frogs spend their whole lives on the forest floor and never enter the water. They don't need to, because the air is so wet. Only a few live in or near ponds and streams.

6

Most rain forest frogs eat insects. There are so many crickets, moths, termites, ants, and other insects in the forest that frogs have plenty to eat.

Big frogs may go beyond eating insects. Some large "horned frogs" have green and brown bodies that blend perfectly with the forest floor. These frogs don't hunt for food. They just sit and wait. They can eat almost anything that comes their way, even mice and small rats.

9

The disguise of the horned frogs also protects them from becoming food for larger animals. Many small frogs protect themselves by hiding, too. Some have brown patterns that disguise them on tree trunks or among dead leaves.

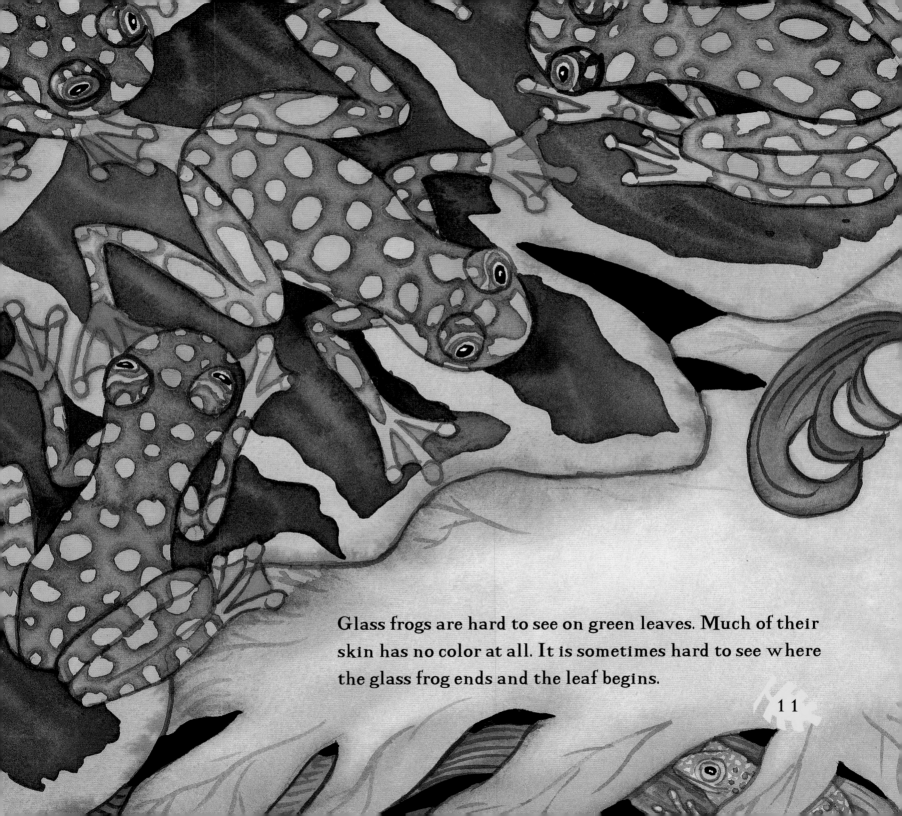

Glass frogs are hard to see on green leaves. Much of their skin has no color at all. It is sometimes hard to see where the glass frog ends and the leaf begins.

11

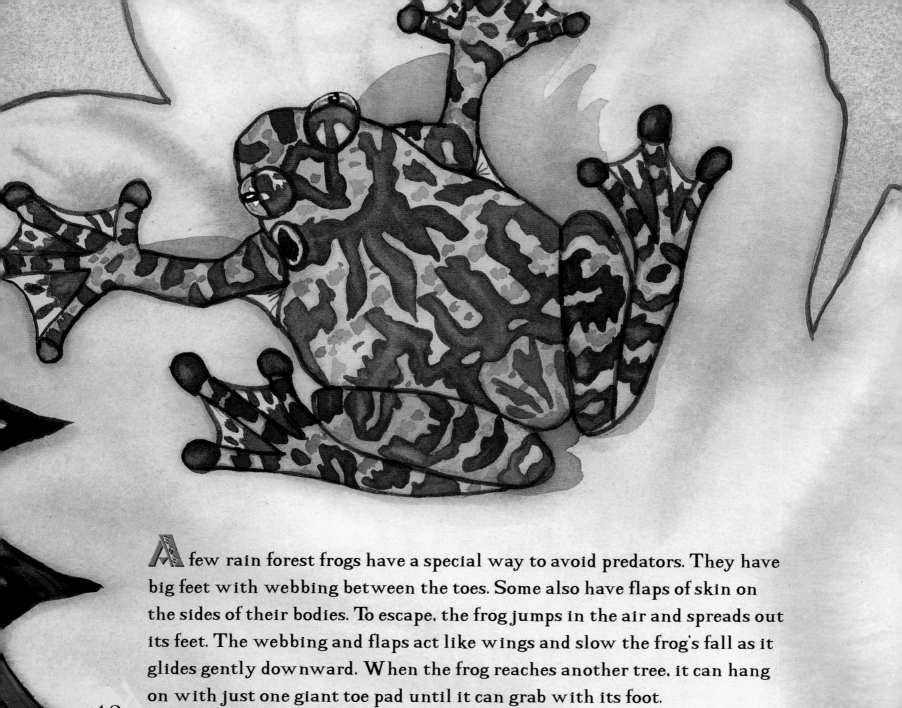

few rain forest frogs have a special way to avoid predators. They have big feet with webbing between the toes. Some also have flaps of skin on the sides of their bodies. To escape, the frog jumps in the air and spreads out its feet. The webbing and flaps act like wings and slow the frog's fall as it glides gently downward. When the frog reaches another tree, it can hang on with just one giant toe pad until it can grab with its foot.

12

Poison dart frogs don't need to hide or escape. They hop fearlessly about on the forest floor during the day. Their bright colors warn predators, "Don't touch me." Only a few animals can eat them, because their skin contains bitter-tasting chemicals. Some of these chemicals are very poisonous.

14

Native hunters in Colombia roll the tips of their blowgun darts onto the skin of certain poison dart frogs. The poison will last for about a year. The hunters use it to kill game, but they must be very careful. The skin of one small frog can contain enough poison to kill more than a hundred people.

15

At mating time, female frogs recognize the special croaking sound of their own species and follow it to find mates. Once the male and female are together, he fertilizes the eggs as she lays them.

16

Many rain forest
frogs do not lay their eggs in
the water. The eggs of some frogs
are protected by foam nests along the
water's edge or on overhanging leaves. The
foam keeps the eggs moist and helps protect
them from predators. Often, the tadpoles
hatch within the foam, and rain carries
them into the water.

17

Tadpoles eat lots of food and grow fast. When a tadpole gets big enough, hind legs begin to grow. Then come the front legs, and the tadpole's tail starts to shrink. As its legs grow, the tadpole changes from an animal that gets oxygen from the water to one that breathes air. Its round mouth grows into a wide frog mouth, and its eyes bulge up. Now it is a tiny frog and can leave the water.

19

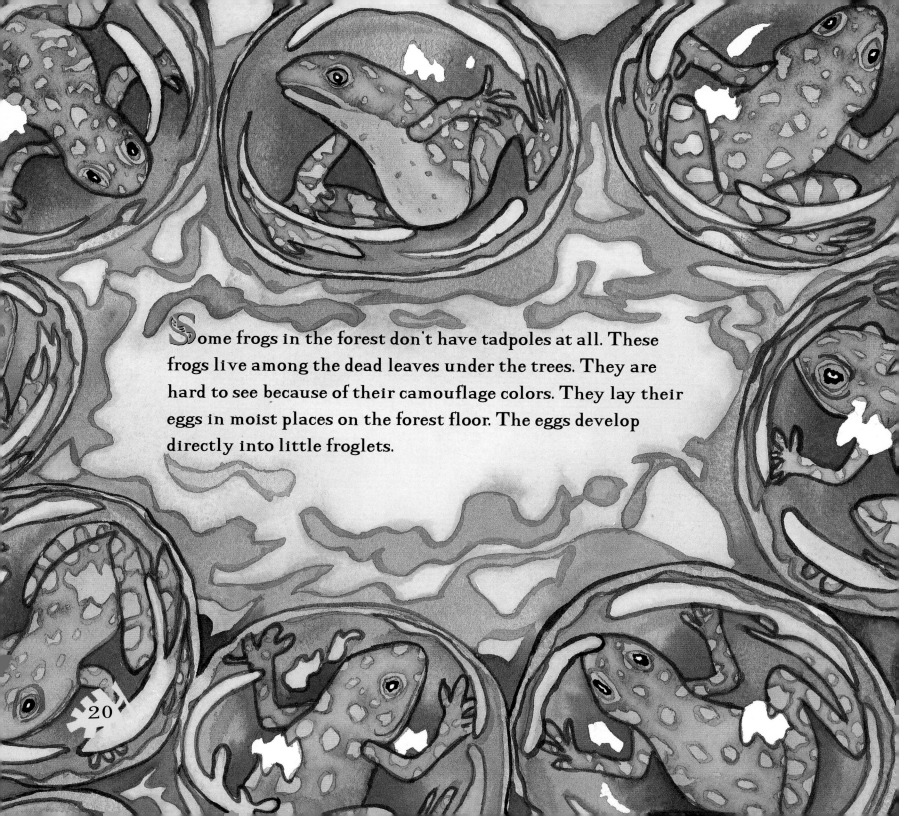

Some frogs in the forest don't have tadpoles at all. These frogs live among the dead leaves under the trees. They are hard to see because of their camouflage colors. They lay their eggs in moist places on the forest floor. The eggs develop directly into little froglets.

20

Some frogs that live high in the trees carry their eggs in
pouches on their backs. The eggs develop while safely protected
on their mother's back. When the little frogs are ready to hatch,
the pouch splits open along the center, and the youngsters
struggle out into the world.

21

Poison dart frogs have their own way of reproducing. Each male has his own territory on the forest floor. With his croaking, he warns other males to stay away. If another male challenges him, they wrestle to find out which is stronger. The wrestling match may last an hour or more.

When a female joins a male for mating, he leads her to
a good place to lay a small batch of eggs.

After the eggs hatch, one parent carries the tadpoles on its back to a small puddle of water. The puddle might be on the forest floor or in a plant. Many rain forest plants store water in the space where the leaves join the stem or right in their center. These small puddles are home to a great variety of life, from bacteria to mosquito larvae. Some of these creatures can be food for the tadpoles.

A few species of poison dart frogs don't leave their tadpoles to find food on their own. The female puts each of her tadpoles into a different puddle. Every few days, she goes back to each puddle and lays infertile eggs (eggs that won't hatch) to feed her tadpoles.

25

The chemicals in poison dart frog skin are very interesting to scientists. Like other poisons, they can be useful as medicine in small doses. One chemical from poison dart frog skin is a more powerful painkiller than morphine. Others could be used as heart-attack medicines.

27

Frogs need homes to live in.
When forests are cut down,
frogs and other animals have no
place to live, so they die out. Frogs
that live in a limited area are especially
threatened. The blue poison frog, for
example, is found only in small parts of forest
in the South American country of Suriname. If its
home is destroyed by people harvesting wood,
this frog will become
extinct.

28

Frogs have been on Earth for more than 150 million years. But today, frogs are disappearing quickly from some parts of the planet. No one is sure why. Some fear that the increase in ultraviolet light reaching Earth may be to blame. Whatever is killing frogs could be a danger for other forms of life, too. Scientists are working hard to understand what is happening, so that the beauty and usefulness of frogs will always be with us.

INDEX

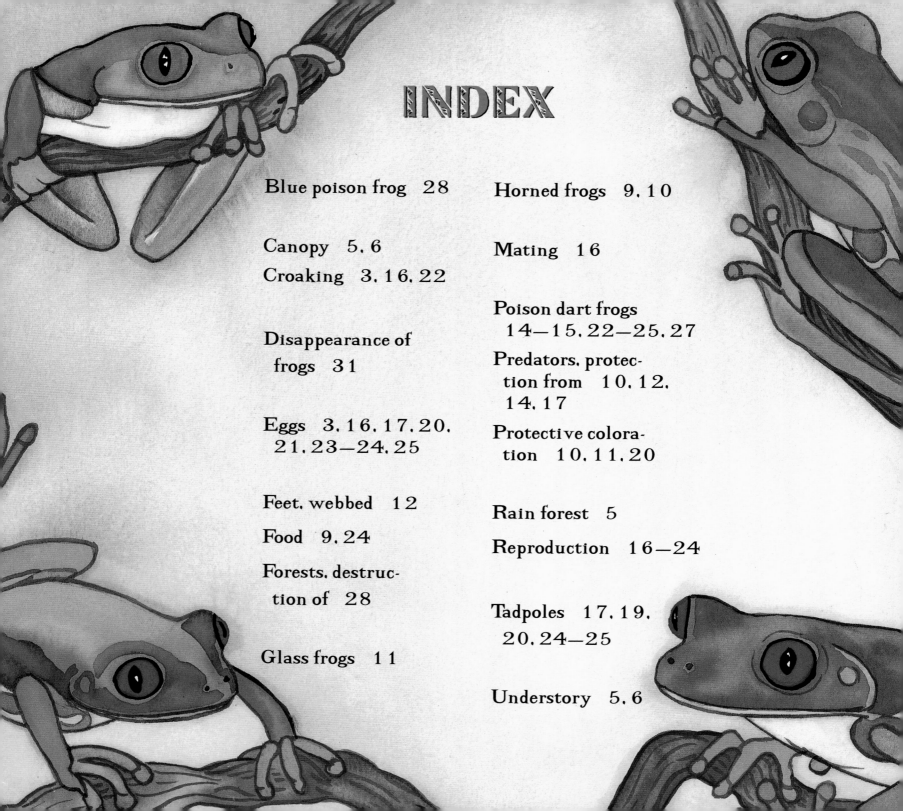